Dare to Dream

Preview Book

Dare to Dream
Series Components

Dare to Dream:
Creating a God-Sized Mission Statement for Your Life
978-1-4267-7577-2

Dare to Dream
DVD
978-1-4267-7578-9

Dare to Dream
Video Leader Guide
978-1-4267-7579-6

Dare to Dream
Youth Book
978-1-4267-7580-2

Dare to Dream
Youth DVD
978-1-4267-7582-6

Dare to Dream
Children's Leader Guide
978-1-4267-7581-9

Dare to Dream
Preview Book
978-1-4267-7583-3

Mike Slaughter

Dare to Dream

Preview Book

Abingdon Press
Nashville

Dare to Dream:
Preview Book

Copyright © 2013 by Abingdon Press

All rights reserved.

This book is printed on acid-free paper.

ISBN 978-1-4267-7583-3

13 14 15 16 17 18 19 20 21 22—10 9 8 7 6 5 4 3 2 1

MANUFACTURED IN THE UNITED STATES OF AMERICA

Contents

Introduction

How many times have you heard yourself saying, "Someday I'm going to . . . "? Fill in the blank.

Sound familiar? I believe "someday" is the enemy to the gift of today. "Someday" is daydreaming. Before Jesus Christ transformed my life, I did a whole lot of daydreaming. I used to sit in school, stare out the window, and daydream hour after hour. I had the grades to prove it. But daydreaming and God-dreaming are not the same thing. Daydreaming is putting off today what you dream of for tomorrow. God-dreaming means putting feet to faith.

This little preview book is an introduction to my book and series *Dare to Dream: Creating a God-Sized Mission Statement for Your Life*. In six short chapters, this preview book will give you a glimpse of the book and series, in which you will explore God's dream for you and create a life mission statement.

I wrote *Dare to Dream* with three purposes in mind. First, I want to wake you up to the God-dream inside of you. You have one; I am sure you do. Jesus gave the dream to you when he came into your life. Second, I want to help you develop a life mission statement. You may have life goals, but that's not the same. Goals can change by season or circumstance, but a life mission statement never changes. Third, I want to challenge you to commit fully to your God-directed life mission, starting now. Today is the day to seize the present of the presence!

1

Dreaming the Dream

Jacob left Beer-sheba and set out for Haran. He reached a certain place and spent the night there. When the sun had set, he took one of the stones at that place and put it near his head. Then he lay down there. He dreamed and saw a raised staircase, its foundation on earth and its top touching the sky, and God's messengers were ascending and descending on it. Suddenly the LORD was standing on it and saying, "I am the LORD, the God of your father Abraham and the God of Isaac."

Genesis 28:10-13

1

Dreaming the Dream

Each year when New Year's Day rolls around, many of us find ourselves setting goals or resolutions for the new year. Lose weight, be on time for work, hit the gym three times a week, reduce yelling at the kids by 25 percent weekly and never yell on Sundays—the list goes on. Those might all be worthwhile goals, but we seriously need to ask ourselves: Am I thinking too small? Am I living the "just get by" plan, or is there a greater God-dream that, if lived to the fullest, could permeate and inform every move I make?

In *Dare to Dream* you will seek to discern God's purpose for your life, and you will create a life mission statement based on it. You might ask, "How will I recognize my God-dream when I see it?

As an example of a God-dream, let's take a look at the story of Jacob in the Old Testament. Jacob eventually became a wealthy, successful businessperson in the field of animal husbandry. In Genesis 28, however, he was on the lam (pun intended). Actually, Jacob had just deceived his elderly father Isaac into giving him the inheritance intended for his older brother Esau. Understandably, Esau was unhappy about his brother's deception, so their parents sent Jacob to stay with extended family for his own safety. We read, starting in Genesis 28:10, that Jacob left Beer-sheba and set out for Haran, about a 750-mile trip. Keep in mind that 750 miles was a significant journey in a time without any kind of motorized transportation.

As the night approached, Jacob stopped at a nondescript place, which the Scripture doesn't even give a name. Jacob took a stone lying nearby and placed it under his head in an attempt to sleep. This would certainly be the ideal setup for a night of restless sleep. Do you ever have restless nights? Note that God often uses restlessness in our lives to get our attention and create change, especially when we find ourselves in a difficult situation. In his sleep, Jacob dreamed that he saw a stairway resting on the earth, its top reaching to heaven, with angels ascending and descending on it. In practical terms that dream doesn't make much sense. We know logically that there are no staircases or ladders connecting earth and heaven. But think about your dreams. How many of those at first don't seem to make sense?

In verses 13 and 14, Jacob saw God standing on the staircase, promising Jacob and his descendants the land on which Jacob was resting. God also promised that Jacob's offspring would become as numerous as the "dust of the earth" and that God would protect Jacob, never leaving him until the promise was fulfilled. Genesis 28:16-17 describes Jacob's reaction:

> When Jacob woke from his sleep, he thought to himself, The LORD is definitely in this place, but I didn't know it. He was terrified and thought, This sacred place

is awesome. It's none other than God's house and the entrance to heaven.

As he did for Jacob, God has created for each of us a unique part to play in his creative plan. God is trying to get our attention so we can live that plan, and God will not leave us until the plan is fulfilled in our lives. That is what I call "living the dream," and it is what I am experiencing in my own life. I am living God's dream for me, and I don't want you to miss yours! Life is too short.

So Jacob had this crazy dream with staircases and angels, but it did have a point. Because of the dream, Jacob realized that God was a powerful presence to whom Jacob had previously been oblivious. Jacob then *knew* that God was with him.

Maybe your "crazy" dreams also have a point. I believe our dreams may be the narrowest crossing between heaven and earth, between spiritual and physical, between supernatural and natural. In early Christian and Jewish traditions, people didn't believe that heaven and earth were far away but existed right next to each other. Dreams provide a bridge between our conscious and subconscious. Because of the busyness and noise of our daily routines and concerns, our subconscious most often comes into play when we are asleep. Through dreams, we can begin to see to the other side.

Of course, God also can speak to us through visions when we are awake. Let's take a look at Acts 9:10-12:

> In Damascus there was a certain disciple named Ananias. The Lord spoke to him in a vision, "Ananias!" He answered, "Yes, Lord." The Lord instructed him, "Go to Judas' house on Straight Street and ask for a man from Tarsus named Saul. He is praying. In a vision he has seen a man named Ananias enter and put his hands on him to restore his sight."

It's interesting how specific this vision is. Have you ever been sitting in your house watching

TV or totally engrossed in what you were doing, only to have a person's name pop into your head? There's a chance that such thoughts may come from God. If the thought is good or appropriate, then I believe it's from God. I know that whenever it happens to me, no matter how involved I am in what I am doing, I need to get up and call that person or take the action that God has brought to mind. These types of experiences are visions. It's the Holy Spirit moving, and there is nothing more important for me to do at that moment than respond. God speaks through dreams when we are asleep, and God speaks through visions when we are awake.

My goal in the pages ahead is to awaken the God-dream in you and unlock the gift of what it means to live that dream—a dream that honors God, blesses others, and brings you joy.

2

Discovering Your Birthright

He gave some apostles, some prophets, some evangelists, and some pastors and teachers. His purpose was to equip God's people for the work of serving and building up the body of Christ until we all reach the unity of faith and knowledge of God's Son. God's goal is for us to become mature adults—to be fully grown, measured by the standard of the fullness of Christ.

Ephesians 4:11-13

2

Discovering Your Birthright

When God puts a dream inside you, it's not just for you. A God-dream will honor God and bless other people in tangible ways. It's your birthright. Let's explore how we discover our birthright as we lean fully into the purpose for which we've been created.

We talked in Chapter 1 about Jacob and his dream. In the dream he saw a staircase, or ladder, with angels going up and down. Most important, though, was what Jacob saw at the top of the ladder. It was God. Stop for a moment and ask yourself what's at the top of your ladder. Your life dreams will be limited by the ceiling of your life pictures. What limitations are your life pictures placing on you?

Let's continue Jacob's story:

> After Jacob got up early in the morning, he took the stone that he had put near his head, set it up as a sacred pillar, and poured oil on the top of it. He named that sacred place Bethel. (Genesis 28:18-19)

At that point, God had really gotten Jacob's attention, and Jacob was beginning to recognize his God-dream. Jacob then made a promise to God:

> "If God is with me and protects me on this trip I'm taking, and gives me bread to eat and clothes to wear, and I return safely to my father's household, then the LORD will be my God. This stone that I've set up as a sacred pillar will be God's house, and of everything you give me I will give a tenth back to you." (vv. 20-22)

I love God's patience. Did you notice all "ifs" and "buts" implied in Jacob's response? The Lord would be his God *if* Jacob was protected, got food to eat and clothes to wear, made it back to his father in one piece, and on and on. There were so many conditions to his commitment! To move forward, Jacob would have to lose his "big buts," which we will talk about in Chapter 4. For now, though, Jacob was at least beginning to understand God had a dream for him that was greater than being a successful herder.

In fact, God had a change-the-world purpose not just for Jacob's life but for all our lives before we were born. You might think, "Who, me?" But the Book of Jeremiah proclaims, "I know the plans I have in mind for you, declares the LORD" (Jeremiah 29:11). And Jesus said, "I assure you that whoever believes in me will do the works that I do. They will do even greater works than these" (John 14:12).

Don't let the scope of your dreams be limited by the ceiling of your life pictures! Many of us initially respond as Moses did when God told him (paraphrase of Exodus 3:7-11), "I hear the cries of my children who are in bondage in Egypt, and I'm going to send you." Moses responded, "Who am I that you would send me? There are far more gifted people. There are better people. There are people who don't struggle in their faith the way I do, Lord. There are people who demonstrate a higher character level than I do, Lord." Sound familiar?

But here's the thing: God doesn't make mistakes. When you were created, God had a distinct plan for your life. God won't back out of it. God won't quit. Jacob is a perfect example. Jacob's very name, according to Esau in Genesis 27:36, meant what most of us today would call identity theft. He had taken the birthright and blessing of his brother and was on the run, fearing retribution. And yet God had a great dream for Jacob's life.

Do you know what your own birthright is? Ephesians 4:11 indicates that God has equipped people to be apostles, prophets, evangelists, pastors, and teachers. How many people reading this book have those life purposes and don't even know it? Who is at the top of your ladder?

What Jacob discovered when he saw God at the top of the ladder in his dream was a revelation of God's presence. Jacob discovered his true birthright. It wasn't being a con man who steals other people's identities. Rather, God created him for a unique mission on earth. The mission, which had a lot of "ifs" and "buts," would need some clarifying. But God kept working on him. In Genesis 32, God changed his name from Jacob, con man, to Israel, which means one who struggles with God.

Note what Jacob did in Genesis 28:18 after his dream: "After Jacob got up early in the morning, he took the stone that he had put near his head, set it up as a sacred pillar, and poured oil on the top of it." In the Old Testament, when people had visions of God, they would sometimes take a stone and, to commemorate the experience, put it in a nearby place where they regularly traveled or walked.

Today, for you and me, we might consider placing an object that acts as a memorial stone in our office, factory, or home as a reminder of the God-mission in our lives. When I walk out of my office at night, I might be tired, cranky, and hungry. But then I see my memorial stone. It reminds me of the work for which I was sent. It keeps me from getting so distracted by the daily grind of my day job that I'm not finishing my God-purpose.

My life mission statement serves as my memorial stone. It is different from my goals, which may change with the season or circumstance. It describes my God-purpose and is what I will use in saying to the Father on Judgment Day, "I have finished the work that you called me to do."

God has created you for a change-the-world purpose. You need to uncover it. The last thing you want to do is stand before the Father on Judgment Day and say, "I didn't even know what my life purpose was."

3

Your Burning Bush

When the Lord *saw that he was coming to look, God called to him out of the bush, "Moses, Moses!"*

Moses said, "I'm here."

Then the Lord *said, "Don't come any closer! Take off your sandals, because you are standing on holy ground." He continued, "I am the God of your father, Abraham's God, Isaac's God, and Jacob's God." Moses hid his face because he was afraid to look at God.*

Exodus 3:4-6

3

Your Burning Bush

You have been created to be a part of God's redemptive mission in the world. You weren't sent to Planet Earth just to eat food and make a living; you were meant to experience and carry out God's dream. Part of identifying that dream is to encounter a burning bush.

Let's look at how it happened for Moses in Exodus 3. By that time, Moses had been living in the land of Midian for forty years, taking care of his father-in-law's flock. One day he was tending the sheep near Horeb, a place known as the "mountain of God," when he spotted a bush that appeared to be on fire and yet wasn't being burned up. Not surprisingly, that got Moses' attention, so he stopped to check it out.

The Lord spoke to him from within the bush, directing Moses to remove his sandals because he was standing on holy ground. Frightened, Moses hid his face. But God went on: "The cry of the Israelites has now come to me; I have also seen how the Egyptians oppress them. So come, I will send you to Pharaoh to bring my people, the Israelites, out of Egypt" (Exodus 3:9-10 NRSV).

Moses encountered a burning bush, and you will too if you look for it. The ultimate hunger, thirst, and passion that all of us feel is to find the reason we were created. Even though we can't always name that hunger, and we often try to satisfy it with other things, all of us want to know our life purpose.

We can learn a lot about discovering our life purpose by studying the story of Moses. It reveals three life stages that all of us go through in the process of finding our purpose. For Moses, those life stages just happened to come in three segments of forty years each.

Stage 1: Empire Building

The first forty years of Moses' life demonstrated what I call self-ascension, or empire building. Moses was born a Hebrew slave, but Pharaoh had issued a mandate at the time of his birth to kill all Hebrew babies. Pharaoh feared the Hebrews were becoming too populous and worried about what would happen if the slaves ever decided to revolt. So Moses' mother took a basket, covered it with pitch, and hid the handcrafted lifeboat in the reeds of the Nile River with Moses inside. Pharaoh's daughter found the baby along the shore and adopted him as her own. From an early age Moses was consumed by his role as prince of Egypt and what it would mean for him to lead the powerful empire. Using the metaphor of ladder climbing, we can say that during this first stage on the bottom rungs, Moses was completely absorbed by his own wants and needs.

All of us go through this stage. We attend school to educate ourselves for the future, then go off to college or start a career. Relationships happen. Some of us marry and have a family. At this stage we aren't usually asking, "God, what is your will for my life?" We are more focused on getting God to bless our endeavors, praying, "Oh God, if I could only get a date with that girl" or "If I could only get that promotion, God." These are "God bless me" prayers. Everything is about ladder climbing. In this stage, if we ask ourselves who is at the top of our ladder and answer truthfully, it usually isn't God, even if we claim to believe in God. We aren't really looking for God's will, but instead we are trying to make God's will fit into and support our own.

Stage 2: Disillusionment

In the second stage we find disillusionment, which usually is initiated by crisis. For Moses, the crisis happened at age forty, and it had to do with anger-management issues. Moses had been given a name that was Egyptian, not Hebrew, but he still had a distant memory of his Hebrew ancestry. One day when he was out supervising workers, he saw the slave masters beating Hebrew slaves. Moses became so furious at one slave master that he killed him. Now, even if you were prince of Egypt you didn't kill an Egyptian citizen. Moses had to flee, and he became a sheepherder in the land of Midian, where he lived and worked for the next forty years of his life. No doubt, being a sheepherder was tremendously different from being the prince of Egypt. A change like that will get your attention.

The disillusionment that Moses experienced was what today we might call a midlife crisis. Perhaps at first you thought marriage would be the best thing ever, that your spouse would satisfy your deep hunger and thirst for fulfillment and significance. Then you reached the top of that particular ladder only to discover that the void was still there. That's when some of us start extramarital affairs, get divorced, or simply begin to live passionless, parallel existences with our spouses.

For others of us, disillusionment may come through the loss of a job. We've worked hard and done everything right, and suddenly we are laid off, asking, "Why has this happened to me?" Or disillusionment may come through sickness or loss. Life presents so many tragedies, and as a pastor I am exposed to a lot of them.

When we hit Stage 2, the prayer is no longer "God bless me." Instead, the prayer is "God save me." It's at this point when we are most receptive to a burning bush, allowing us to move into Stage 3.

Stage 3: A Fire That Won't Burn Out

Let's return to the moment when Moses saw the burning bush.

> There the angel of the Lord appeared to him in a flame of fire out of a bush; he looked, and the bush was blazing, yet it was not consumed. Then Moses said, "I must turn aside and look at this great sight, and see why the bush is not burned up." (Exodus 3:2-3 NRSV)

Isn't it interesting that the bush wasn't burned up by the fire? When you encounter your burning bush—a defining event that leads you to your life purpose—it creates a fire in you that will not burn out. A true God-purpose will not burn you out or burn you up.

Notice that when Moses saw the burning bush he said, "I must turn aside." It's true for all of us. We must turn away from dull daily routines and lackluster lives—from the "same old, same old" that we have been doing year after year. When we change our priorities and replace what's at the top of our ladder, we are in Stage 3. We understand then, as Moses did, that no matter where our feet happen to be planted, we are standing on holy ground.

God does not invest in our personal agendas. He has called us to invest in his redemptive plan. Stage 1 is "Bless me." Stage 2 is "Save me." Stage 3 is "Use me."

4

Lose Your Big Buts

But Moses said to God, "Who am I to go to Pharaoh and to bring the Israelites out of Egypt?"

God said, "I'll be with you. And this will show you that I'm the one who sent you. After you bring the people out of Egypt, you will come back here and worship God on this mountain."

Exodus 3:11-12

4

Lose Your Big Buts

Excuses, excuses—we all have them. "*But* I don't have the right kind of education." "*But* I'm too old to live that dream." "*But* the money just isn't there." "*But* that decision feels way too risky." "*But* I'm just one ordinary person."

Frankly, no dream worth pursuing will come easily. There will be obstacles, and there will be excuses—what I call our "big buts." If we are to fulfill God's dream for our lives, we have to lose our big buts, or at least downsize them.

Let's return to the story of Moses in Exodus 3. Moses had just had a God vision, a burning bush experience. Moses was eighty years old, and God told Moses to leave the land of Midian and return to Egypt, where Moses would take on the Pharaoh and his armies and deliver tens of thousands of people from slavery. (Exodus 12:37 tells us the Israelites numbered at least 600,000, not counting the children.) As you can imagine, Moses came up with a boatload of "buts."

I'm Not Qualified

The first big but is in Exodus 3:11. "But Moses said to God, 'Who am I to go to Pharaoh and to bring the Israelites out of Egypt?'" In other words, "God, I'm not qualified."

Do you ever say that to God? Well, rest assured that if you *do* feel qualified, then your mission is not big enough. To put it another way, if you are only doing things you think you can accomplish, then you haven't discovered your life mission. God wants to challenge you and stretch you. God's true purpose for you probably will feel impossible. If that seems harsh, just remember: God said, "I'll be with you" (Exodus 3:12).

I'm Spiritually Unfit

The second big but is in verse 13: "But Moses said to God, 'If I now come to the Israelites and say to them, "The God of your ancestors has sent me to you," they are going to ask me, "What's this God's name?" What am I supposed to say to them?'" In other words, "But God, I'm spiritually unfit. I'm spiritually ill-prepared. I'm spiritually illiterate."

Many of us look at Moses and think he had it together—that he had an intimate relationship with God. But he didn't really know who God was. Think about it: For the first forty years of Moses' life, he was exposed to the pantheon of Egyptian gods, and as a prince of Egypt he would have been expected to study them all. Then for the next forty years of his life, Moses was in Midian, where his father-in-law was a priest; the Midianites were also polytheistic. Moses probably believed there were all kinds of gods, many of which he had studied and even worshipped. In essence he was asking God, "Which one are you? What am I supposed to tell the people when they ask me your name?"

No One Will Believe Me

The third big but is found in Exodus 4:1. Moses asked God, "But what if they don't believe me or pay attention to me? They might say to me, 'The Lord didn't appear to you!'" In other words, "But God, what if I can't convince them? These people know who I am. I lack credibility."

Moses also had a past reputation to worry about. Remember, he fled Egypt after murdering an Egyptian citizen. Moses believed if he went back, he would have all the credibility of a murderer. Moses, like all of us, doubted what God could accomplish through him. We base those expectations on our own understanding of our limitations and failures, and also on other people's opinions.

I'm Afraid

The fourth big but is in Exodus 4:10. Moses told God, "My Lord, I've never been able to speak well, not yesterday, not the day before, and certainly not now since you've been talking to your servant. I have a slow mouth and a thick tongue." In other words, "I stumble over my words. I'm afraid to speak in front of people."

Excuses aren't always something we come up with on our own. Sometimes we claim self-limiting beliefs that are assigned to us by others. What self-limiting beliefs do you need to shed? "He's not college material." "She doesn't have the talent for that." "She isn't the right color (or creed or age)." Naysayers limit our goals and create fear that at worst is paralyzing and at best prevents us from living out the fullness of God's dream for our lives. An event later in Moses' story provides a great example of how listening to the wrong folks can create fear, paralysis, and excuses for not living out our God-dream.

About a year after Moses led the Israelites out of Egypt, he sent twelve people ahead of everyone else to check out the Promised Land. He said:

> "Go up there into the arid southern plain and into the mountains. You must inspect the land. What is it like? Are the people who live in it strong or weak, few or many? Is the land in which they live good or bad? Are the towns in which

they live camps or fortresses? Is the land rich or poor? Are there trees in it or not? Be courageous and bring back the land's fruit." (Numbers 13:17-20)

Jumping ahead to verse 27, we see that the people came back with a report that met Moses' expectations: "We entered the land to which you sent us. It's actually full of milk and honey, and this is its fruit." If only they had stopped there! But ten of the twelve people (all but Joshua and Caleb) continued their report in verses 28-33:

"There are, however, powerful people who live in the land. . . . The land that we crossed over to explore is a land that devours its residents. All the people we saw in it are huge men. We saw there the Nephilim (the descendants of Anak come from the Nephilim). We saw ourselves as grasshoppers, and that's how we appeared to them."

As a result of that negative report, the children of Israel became afraid and wandered the desert for another thirty-nine years.

Besides being careful who you listen to, be careful what you say. During that thirty-nine-year period, hundreds of thousands of Israelites died in the wilderness as a result of the ten people's negativity and the fear it fostered. That's why my life rule is: speak faith when you feel futility. This doesn't mean the road to God's dream will be easy. The future doesn't just stand there waving us in. I don't want to be one of the ten who raised the white flag of surrender. I want to stand with Joshua and Caleb, the two who lifted the flag of God's promise and said in Numbers 13:30: "We must go up and take possession of it, because we are more than able to do it."

5

What Is in Your Hand?

The LORD said to him, "What's that in your hand?"

Moses replied, "A shepherd's rod."

The LORD said, "Throw it down on the ground." So Moses threw it on the ground, and it turned into a snake. Moses jumped back from it. Then the LORD said to Moses, "Reach out and grab the snake by the tail." So Moses reached out and grabbed it, and it turned back into a rod in his hand. "Do this so that they will believe that the LORD, the God of their ancestors, Abraham's God, Isaac's God, and Jacob's God has in fact appeared to you."

Exodus 4:2-5

5

What Is in Your Hand?

When Moses encountered his burning bush, it exposed his lack of confidence and his perception of his own resources as limited. But then God asked him a question that became the catalyst for all the resources Moses could ever possibly need. It's time for us to lay hold of the same confidence and provision as we ask ourselves that very same question: What is in your hand?

Psalm 139 declares that every one of us has been intricately woven together in our mother's womb, fearfully and wonderfully made. God has a purpose for each of us, and we have been created with everything needed to fulfill that purpose. Life is short. We will soon stand before God on Judgment Day, and I want all of us to be able to say, "Father, I have finished the work that you sent me to do." We just have to realize that everything we need, we already have.

Let's return to Exodus 4, where we were examining Moses' burning-bush experience. Moses was eighty years old when he learned his mission through the burning bush; thank God he discovered it before he died! Moses ran through his litany of "big buts," but God wasn't about to let him off the hook.

Then, in Exodus 4:2, God asked Moses the critical question: "What's that in your hand?" Moses answered, "A shepherd's rod"—basically a staff, a stick. You know that Moses had to be thinking, "What am I going to do with a stick?" After asking the question, the Lord gave a command: "Throw it down on the ground" (v. 3). So Moses threw it on the ground. It became a snake! What did Moses do? He "jumped back from it"; in other words, he ran or at least thought of running. Looking at our own lives, how often do we run from the work that God is trying to accomplish through us? But God wasn't through with Moses yet:

Then the LORD said to Moses, "Reach out and grab the snake by the tail." So Moses reached out and grabbed it, and it turned back into a rod in his hand. "Do this so that they will believe that the LORD, the God of their ancestors, Abraham's God, Isaac's God, and Jacob's God has in fact appeared to you." (v. 4-5)

Now, the problem is that you and I tend to focus on what we don't have versus what we do have. Please hear me: In God, everything that you need you have already been given. In God, all the resources required to accomplish the mission you were created for you already possess. God uses our ordinary gifts, talents, and life experiences, which you and I often take for granted, to fulfill his dream for us.

Are you scratching your head, unsure as to which gifts and talents you have and are supposed to use? Three key questions will help you identify them.

The Gifts of My Head

The first question is: "What are the gifts of my head?" In other words, what do you know a lot about? What do you know more about than a lot of people around you? Let me share one example from my own life.

As a kid I was forced to go to church, and I observed a great deal about why church didn't relate to unchurched people. It was behind-numbingly boring!

I loved what the wider culture had to offer. I enjoyed the music and movies; I liked to hang out in clubs. Even today I struggle to listen to Christian radio stations because the music is so boring. It repeats over and over again, "We love you, Jesus" and "Thank you, Jesus, for loving us." Now, all of that is certainly true, but it is delivered in a manner that can feel trivial and trite.

From an early age I knew and understood why the church felt irrelevant to the unchurched people I knew. I really got it. Later, as a pastor, I used that head knowledge to avoid being that kind of church.

The Gifts of My Hands

The second question to ask is: "What are the gifts of my hands?" What do you do better than a lot of people around you?

The one thing I did really well, even as a kid, was to start new things that would grow and attract other people. When I was a junior in high school, I played guitar in a rock band. I have a picture of me performing that year at a high school dance. I am not too hard to pick out: I am the only white face in the crowd. Being in that band gave me the idea to start a club where teens could come and dance. I found a place, opened a club, and started making up to eighty dollars a night. Back in the 1960s that was a lot of money for a sixteen-year-old kid. I had a talent for starting new things that would attract people and even make money. Do you see how God used this? What God awakened in my life was the ability to start things that would grow and attract people to come and join in the rhythm of God's big dance.

God was also working on something else in my life at the same time—my drive to stand up and speak out against racism, sexism, and any other "ism" that divides or denigrates. The race riots of 1968 had a huge impact on my life and my future understanding. Do you see how God can use all your experiences and the gifts of your hands?

The Passion of My Heart

The third question is: "What is the passion of my heart?"

I was most passionate about connecting students to Jesus Christ. If Jesus could change our lives, he could change our high school. And if he could change our high school, he could change our community. And if he could change our community, he could change our world. That passion is still burning. Burning bushes don't go out. Every year, I return to my alma mater, North College Hill High School in Cincinnati, to hold assemblies. My wife Carolyn and I give a few scholarships each year to high-potential students.

These three key questions will help you discover what is in your hand: What are the gifts of my head? What are the gifts of my hands? What is the passion of my heart?

We are born to and wired for a God-purpose in the world. God's question to you is: "What is in your hand?" Everything you need has already been given to you. Then, as with Moses and his staff, God commands you to throw it on the ground. Think about that for a minute. It's a strong directive. God didn't say, "Why don't you gently place it on the ground?" Many times we think, "Maybe I won't really throw it. I'll just keep my hand on it, in case this doesn't work out." I hear people say many times, "Well, I knew I was not supposed to sit around and only take. I knew I was supposed to move out and do. But then it got a little risky and cost more money or time than I thought." With that kind of thinking, we snatch the gift or talent back out of God's hand again, because we never really released it for his purposes.

Once you recognize what is in your hand, you then have to release it to increase it. You have to take what you have been given by God and release it into God's hand. Then you don't take it back again until God tells you to. When God does put it back in your hand, it's no longer just a stick; it's God's stick.

6

Perseverance

"The eye is the lamp of the body. Therefore, if your eye is healthy, your whole body will be full of light. But if your eye is bad, you whole body will be full of darkness. If then the light in you is darkness, how terrible that darkness will be! No one can serve two masters. Either you will hate the one and love the other, or you will be loyal to the one and have contempt for the other."

Matthew 6:22-24

6

Perseverance

As we read on in Exodus, we can see that Moses' God-dream was not going to be a walk in the park. But *quit* was not in his vocabulary. What about you? What will become of your God-dream when obstacles appear? And trust me, they will.

Look at Deuteronomy 34, the last chapter in the Bible about Moses' life. Recall that by that time, Moses had had his burning-bush experience as an eighty-year-old man and had accomplished what seemed to be an impossible mission: go to Egypt and deliver the people of Israel from bondage. In Deuteronomy 34 we jump ahead forty years. Start in Deuteronomy 34:1-3 (NIV):

Then Moses climbed Mount Nebo from the plains of Moab to the top of Pisgah, across from Jericho. There the Lord showed him the whole land—from Gilead to Dan, all of Naphtali, the territory of Ephraim and Manasseh, all the land of Judah as far as the Mediterranean Sea, the Negev and the whole region from the Valley of Jericho, the City of Palms, as far as Zoar.

Moses was now 120 years old, but he was still receiving a big vision from God. Many of the people I know who are age sixty and up are looking backward and doing less. Yet at the time of his death, Moses continued to have a forward focus. Now look at verses 4-7:

Then the Lord said to him, "This is the land I promised on oath to Abraham, Isaac and Jacob when I said, 'I will give it to your descendants.' I have let you see it with your eyes, but you will not cross over into it." And Moses the servant of the Lord died there in Moab, as the Lord had said. He buried him in Moab, in the valley opposite Beth Peor, but to this day no one knows where his grave is. Moses was a hundred and twenty years old when he died, yet his eyes were not weak nor his strength gone.

What separates those who do from those who *don't*? We find the key in that final verse. When the Bible refers to Moses' eyes, it doesn't mean his physical eyes; it means his focus and ultimate priority. Moses was successful in his God-dream because he had a sustaining vision.

This is what Jesus meant when he talked about making blind eyes see: bringing vision to the lost, giving them and us the clarity to focus on the "one thing," the God-priority.

Your eyesight, your vision, has to have a clear focus, without distraction, on the one thing, the God-thing. Many of us are too easily distracted; then the picture gets fuzzy, and dreams start to feel unachievable. Jesus pointed out that we can't serve two masters without winding up hating the one and loving the other.

Why is the sustaining vision so critical? Proverbs 29:18 tells us, "When there's no vision, the people get out of control." In other words, if you don't remain focused on your life mission, then you will lack the discipline to complete it. This is what separates success from failure, and those who do from those who don't. We need to have a process for renewing and sustaining that vision.

Moses experienced a multitude of setbacks and frustrations. He went to Pharaoh nine times, yet Pharaoh said he would not let the slaves go free. Pharaoh finally got so upset that he said to Moses in Exodus 10:28, "Get out of here! Make sure you never see my face again, because the next time you see my face you will die." Seems like most people would have gotten the message right then and there. So, what did Moses do? He went back a tenth time.

Moses' setbacks weren't just because of Pharaoh. They came from the Israelites, the very people he had helped. After finally leaving Egypt, they would whine to him, "Oh, Moses! Manna every day! Manna for breakfast, lunch, and supper! We're tired of manna, Moses! How about some meat? How about some chicken? And by the way, the water is terrible. Moses! Moses! Moses!" Do you know people like that? I certainly do.

Perseverance also means remembering who resources our mission. We don't need to have all the resources at the outset of our mission to accomplish what God is calling us to do; the resources will be given at the appointed time. Look at Moses! He set out from Egypt with a city-worth of people and headed into the wilderness. When Moses set out to lead the masses, he didn't wait until he had all the supplies. He didn't rent U-Haul trucks or figure out how much food they would need for forty years—no, he stepped out.

Here is my philosophy of life: Ready, fire, aim. Too many people say: Ready, aim, fire. If you do that, given the speed of our world today, you may miss out. Moses set out, and what did God do? God provided the resources one day at a time. Notice that if the people became fearful and hoarded God's provision instead of releasing it, the manna rotted. They may have been in an arid desert, but God brought water from a rock. Here is what separates success from failure and those who do from those who don't: Successful people have a way of renewing and sustaining the vision so that it is not consumed; it does not burn out or run out.

What our lives come down to can be embodied in one word: *legacy.* Our life mission is what will live beyond us. We will experience the miracles God made for us when we hear and obey what Jesus is saying in our lives. That's the difference between a daydream and a God-dream. A God-dream happens when you put perspiration to inspiration.

I am living my God-dream, and there is nothing sweeter. I hope and pray that you will find God's dream for you and live it to the fullest.

If you liked this preview book, you'll love the series.

Learn more about discovering God's dream for you in the *Dare to Dream* book and series. The book provides more depth and a chance to create a life mission statement. The series also includes a DVD and leader guide for adults, a book and DVD for youth, and a children's leader guide with reproducible handouts.